THE SECRET OF
THE TWENTY-THIRD
PSALM

Reference Notes

The source for this pamphlet is Recording #614-2,
a Joel Goldsmith class from the
1951 First Seattle Series: Tape 1, side 2.
This recording is currently available in audiotape,
CD, or MP3 format at www.joelgoldsmith.com.

Other Titles in This Series

Supply

Metaphysical Healing

Meditation and Prayer

Business and Salesmanship

Ye Are the Light

The Real Teacher and The Seven Steps

Truth

Love and Gratitude

I Am the Vine

The Deep Silence of My Peace

The Fourth Dimension of Life

Contemplative Meditation with Scripture

The Easter of Our Lives

A Lesson to Sam

Protection

The Truth of Being

Wisdoms of the Infinite Way

What Slows Our Spiritual Progress?

THE SECRET OF
THE TWENTY-THIRD
PSALM

Joel S. Goldsmith

Acropolis Books, Publisher
Longboat Key, Florida

The Secret of the Twenty-Third Psalm
by Joel S. Goldsmith

From Chapter 11 of Collected Essays of Joel S. Goldsmith,
© 1986 Thelma McDonald.

Acropolis Books, Inc.
Longboat Key, Florida
www.acropolisbooks.com

Except the Lord build the house,
they labour in vain that build it.

Psalm 127

Illumination dissolves all material ties and binds men together with the golden chains of spiritual understanding; it acknowledges only the leadership of the Christ; it has no ritual or rule but the divine, impersonal universal Love; no other worship than the inner Flame that is ever lit at the shrine of Spirit. This union is the free state of spiritual brotherhood. The only restraint is the discipline of Soul; therefore, we know liberty without license; we are a united universe without physical limits; a divine service to God without ceremony or creed. The illumined walk without fear – by Grace.

From the *The Infinite Way* by Joel S. Goldsmith

THE SECRET OF THE TWENTY-THIRD PSALM

MEDITATION ON PRAYER

IT IS THROUGH our understanding of prayer that we are able to bring the activity of the Kingdom of God, Harmony, Wholeness, into our individual experience.

If prayer, as it is generally understood, were really prayer, the world would be free of sin, disease, death, wars, famine, drought ... all of these things would have disappeared from the earth in the thousands of years that the subject of prayer has been taught. Scripture tells us that if we pray and do not receive an answer, it is because we have been praying amiss and, if we judge by that, the world has been praying amiss for some thousands of years. The question is whether or not we know any more about prayer now.

Our progress in developing a clearer understanding of prayer has been rather slow, and up to the present time it is primarily an advance in the understanding of prayer as it touches upon our individual problems. The great problem of bringing peace on earth ... good will to men ... is still not solved.

So it becomes our work to devote as much time as possible to the study of the subject of prayer ... to meditation upon that subject ... until we come into higher and higher concepts of prayer.

We will know whether or not we are doing that by the results in our experience. If we are touching a higher note in prayer, we will have better health, better wealth ... more of it ... and a greater degree of harmony in all of our experience.

All too often, prayer consists, to too great a degree, of words, statements, quotations ... whereas prayer, itself, actually is wordless. Prayer has NOTHING to do with anything that we voice ... whether in the form of a petition, affirmation, denial or any other form of speech or thought. Rather, prayer is that which we become aware of IN THE SILENCE ... the Word of God uttering Itself within our consciousness.

In other words, we do not pray unless prayer can be understood as a STATE of RECEPTIVITY. Actually, the Word of God is nothing that WE say but, rather, that which God says WITHIN US.

One form of meditation is to quietly consider some idea concerning God ... think upon it or even voice it ... but dwell upon it for only a short time. Then, become receptive and LET the meditation come through from God.

In other words, God does the meditating ... we become aware of the fruits of that meditation.

In an introduction to an old edition of the Bible, we read: "For is the Kingdom of God become words or syllables? Why should we be in bondage to them if we be free?"

IS the Kingdom of God words? IS the Kingdom of God syllables? NO! The Kingdom of God is WITHIN YOU ... and that Kingdom of God must make Itself manifest to you. IT must declare Itself to you ... utter Itself to you ... voice Itself to you ... and so, the Kingdom of God is not YOUR words nor YOUR syllables.

In our prayers, very often we carry around problems and we wonder what form of treatment we could use for this particular problem or that particular problem ... or what form of prayer ... or if there were some greater understanding we could acquire as to HOW to pray.

If you are having that experience, ponder this passage and the realization in it ... "For IS the Kingdom of God become words or syllables?" ... "WHY should we be in bondage to them [that is to the words or syllables] IF we be free?" Scripture teaches that we ARE free ... we are children of God ... if children, then heirs ... if heirs, then joint heirs in Christ with God.

We are ALREADY free. If we were not free, there is no God power that could make us free.

We ARE free, and the entire truth teaching IS, of course, to bring out that realization or revelation of our present freedom ... not to MAKE it so. It would be well for us to remember, with any of the problems now bothering us, that we might just as well NOT be in bondage to words or syllables or statements of truth but be willing to sit a while and let God reveal Its plan TO us ... Its plan FOR us ... TO us.

We find this in the Smith translation of the scriptures, the 19th Psalm: "The heavens are telling the glory of God ... the sky shows forth the work of His hands... . Day unto day pours forth speech... . Night unto night declares knowledge. There is no speech nor are there words ... their voice is not heard, yet their voice goes forth through all the earth and their words ... to the ends of the world."

The last four lines go back to the first, "The Heavens are telling the glory of God." But then it says: "There is no speech nor are there words." And that is true. The heavens are not voicing themselves in words or speech and yet they ARE telling the glory of God.

"And the sky shows forth the work of His hands." And it says: "Their voice is not heard."

Certainly, the sky has no voice and yet it does show forth the work of His hands.

"Yet their voice goes forth," that is, the heavens and the sky and the day and the night ... their voice goes forth without speech ... without syllables ... without words. Their voice goes forth and declares.

And so it is that our entire experience is one that shows forth the glory of God ... it TELLS the glory of God. Our whole experience ... our entire life ... our bodies ... are continuously showing forth the work of His hands.

If, at this moment, our bodies, our health, do not seem to be showing forth that divine harmony, it is ONLY because we have come under the belief that we have health of our own ... bodies of our own ... powers of our own ... instead of realizing that ALL that concerns us in the body, in the purse or in the home is God showing Itself forth, manifesting Its beauties, Its nature and Its character.

The moment we make the transition from the belief that we HAVE health, that we can lose or gain ... the moment that we give up the idea, the belief that we have health that can be improved, and understand that the only health that there is in all the universe is the health of God, manifesting itself as the health of our bodies or being ... then do we come into the realization of this 19th Psalm:

"The heavens are telling the glory of God," and they are doing it without words and without speech.

"The sky shows forth the work of His hands," and it does it without words and without speech.

"Day unto day pours forth speech." Yes, but day unto day does not talk. It only pours forth speech in the sense of pouring forth the harmony of God's being.

"Night unto night declares knowledge." And it does so without voicing it in speech or other impartation of ideas, except through the activity of showing off God's glory.

Now ... ALL that we are and ALL that we hope to be is GOD showing Itself forth as our health ... as our strength ... as all of the good in our experience. Then, let us give up AT ONCE the belief that our health or wealth is dependent upon certain ARRANGEMENTS of words into treatments or prayers, for the Kingdom of God is NOT words or syllables ... the Kingdom of God is already established within YOU.

Give up the belief that your health or your wealth or home can be dependent upon anything other than the activity of God. ONCE you have seen that point ... that it is the activity of God that maintains the harmony of your being ... you will commence to see a new light on the subject of prayer.

PRACTICAL INTERPRETATION OF THE TWENTY-THIRD PSALM

CONSIDER THE 23rd Psalm. Here is a form of prayer that harmonizes most beautifully with the message of The Infinite Way and its idea of prayer.

"The Lord is my Shepherd, I shall not want."
In that statement there is no APPEAL to
God for anything ... there is no TURNING
to God for anything ... there is not even an
EXPECTANCY of GOOD from God. There
IS a POSITIVE statement that "The Lord IS
my Shepherd," and it naturally follows that
"I shall not want."

Think upon that form of prayer. "The Lord
is my Shepherd, I shall not want." There is
no TURNING to God ... no trying to reach
God ... no old-fashioned petition ... not even
the new-style affirmation. There is ONLY the
recognition that since God IS and since God
is MY Shepherd ... my individual shepherd
... guide ... protector ... guard ... maintainer
and sustainer ... because this IS true, "I shall
not want." There is no question at all. There
is confidence ... there is assurance ... "I shall
not want."

There is no seeking for supply ... no attempt to demonstrate supply ... only the calm, clear assurance, "I shall not want." Understand this ... it is utterly impossible to want!

"He maketh me to lie down in green pastures, He leadeth me beside the still waters."

Again, there is no turning to God ... not in any way, shape, manner or form. Not only does He PROVIDE green pastures but (notice this) "He MAKETH me to lie down" in them. It is not a matter of choice as to whether you WANT to lie down in green pastures or not ... nor is it a matter of punishing you for your sins by keeping you out of the green pastures. It is simply that "He MAKETH me to lie down in green pastures."

You should feel a sense of release as you realize that the burden is no longer on your shoulders, to govern yourself, maintain yourself, sustain yourself or even to find the right kind of prayer.

"The Lord is my Shepherd, I shall not want. He maketh me to lie down in green pastures, He leadeth me beside the still waters. He restoreth my soul. He leadeth me in the path of righteousness for His name's sake."

Observe, all the way through, there is no attempt to gain God's favor, no attempt to seek God's goodness, no attempt in any way to reach out for God ... just this constant, confident assurance.

"Yea, though I walk through the valley of the shadow of death, I will fear no evil, for Thou art with me."

This is truly a miracle of prayer. As you have experienced periods of trial and tribulation ... serious illness ... family troubles ... lack

... limitation ... loss of fortune ... has it not seemed natural to feel that SOMEHOW you have become separated from God ... in some manner you had slipped AWAY from God ... for some reason God was not WITH you and thus, having lost contact, you must now get back to God. Now you can see the error of your thinking ...

"Yea, though I walk through the valley of the shadow of death, I will fear no evil, FOR THOU ART WITH ME."

Even as he walks through the valley of the shadow of death, he cannot fear. Yet that is not true of us. We touch that valley of the shadow of death ... or lack and limitation ... or unemployment ... or whatever the error may be ... and we BEGIN to fear.

This fear begins for one reason only ... lack of the full realization that God is going through the valley of the shadow of death with us.

Behold, here, a whole new concept of prayer. We are not trying to GET God to be with us on this trek through the valley of the shadow of death. We are not reaching OUT for God. We are not even trying to have our fears stilled, since this recognition that God walks WITH us doesn't always save us FROM that walk through the valley of the shadow of death, but at least, if we are called upon to FACE the valley of the shadow of death, this statement tells us HE walks through it WITH us ... "THOU ART WITH ME."

If you would just take that one statement and realize ... what difference does it make WHAT the present valley of the shadow of death is ... what difference does it make WHAT particular trial you are going through as long as you KNOW with all the confidence within you ... that God is walking through the valley of the shadow of death WITH you ... GOD is walking through this trial WITH you.

In *Spiritual Interpretation of Scripture* you will find the story of Joseph and his brethren ... Joseph, the pampered and favorite son of his father, who probably expected to go through life very easily, quietly, calmly, with no trials or tribulations ... and probably with no great victories ... since he was the beneficiary of his father's great wealth and favoritism. However, it was not to be that way. Through the jealousy and deep malice of his brethren, Joseph was brought to the pit and thrown in, to be killed or sold into slavery (which was considered worse than death).

Finally, Joseph found himself in Egypt where he worked up from slavery to a responsible position in the household of the ruler. He has just about satisfied himself that now God is WITH him, when suddenly he is thrown into prison. He pleaded innocent but, innocent or not, he is in prison and, according to sense,

AGAIN he is WITHOUT the presence of God as he is left there for several years. After he is freed, he rises, ultimately, to be the virtual ruler of Egypt.

Then the brethren came. They were the ones who had thrown him into the pit ... sold him into slavery ... brought about ALL his troubles. Now they came seeking a favor. They needed food and Joseph had it. Joseph gave it to them.

When the brethren attempt to apologize for their actions and express their sorrow, Joseph reflects the thoughts of David and says, "You did not do these things to me ... God did them. God sent me, before you, into Egypt."

There is a high concept of prayer in that statement. There is a prayer worth remembering. It is not the devil ... it is not mortal mind ... it is not the opposite of

God that brings about man's discords and diseases. It is God, Itself, that walks with man through his trials and temptations to bring him to some major victory, instead of leaving him alone to be just a healthy or wealthy human being, accomplishing nothing in his threescore years or more of life on this plane.

The average person accomplishes very little on earth except make a living and raise a family. As for any REAL contribution to showing forth the Glory of God, the average person has very little to show in that respect.

KNOW THIS ... it is MEANT that we should bring forth spiritual fruitage ... that we should show forth the handiwork of God ... that we should show forth the Glory of God ... but if we are going to rest on just our perfect health or perfect wealth, we are falling short of our true destiny.

Joseph recognized what YOU are going to recognize ... that envy, jealousy, malice, hate, infection, contagion, depressions, changing governments, cannot bring discord or inharmony to you. Only GOD can bring you to a realization of your true identity in one way or another, and while you are going through the fiery furnace, while you are going through the forty years across the desert with Moses or while you are on the cross with Jesus (it does not make any difference what the nature of your trial or tribulation ... they had every kind of them in scripture) at least you can know that GOD is there WITH you, walking through the experience also.

Had God not been with Jesus on the cross, there would have been no resurrection from the tomb and no ascension. Only the Power of God in the consciousness of Jesus could have brought about the resurrection.

Had there been NO God on that forty-year trek with Moses, there would have been no entrance to the Promised Land ... there would have been no freedom for the Hebrews.

Had there been no God with Joseph, there would have been no mounting up from slavery to virtually being the ruler of the great country of Egypt ... and great it was in that day.

Whatever the problem you are facing, try to realize this ... you are NOT going through it alone ... even though it is the valley of the shadow of death, you need fear no evil for GOD is with you. Consider that high concept of prayer ...

"Thy rod and Thy staff they comfort me."

Whatever you are going through, there is a staff to lean upon and there is a rod to keep you in line. There IS some form of discipline.

There IS some form of teaching. There IS some form of spiritual help to lean upon. You must KNOW this with all your knowing and then ACT with complete confidence in that KNOWING.

Elijah nearly forgot that when he was fed by the ravens and the widow and found cakes baked on the stones. He nearly forgot that it was the presence of GOD that provided those things for him ... NOTHING ELSE ... and that they were provided for him so that he, ALSO, might successfully walk through the valley of the shadow of death and finally come to that place where God reveals to him that he has saved out a congregation of seven thousand of those who did not bow their knees to Baal.

For YOU there is a congregation of seven thousand. For YOU there is a SPIRITUAL mission ... a SPIRITUAL purpose on earth

... and the PARTICULAR trial or tribulation through which you may now be going (or a whole series of them, if necessary) is for the sole purpose of leading you to your ultimate demonstration ... something that could NOT have been done without that PARTICULAR trial or tribulation.

This is the way of the cross ... it is the way of the crown ... but notice that the crown comes long after the crucifixion. First the crucifixions come (and many of them), and for that reason the person entering the spiritual path MUST understand that "I come, not to bring peace but a sword ... to divide households," to break up EVERYTHING that would give you ease and comfort in material circumstances and conditions.

There can be no spiritual progress until you have overcome the world. As long as you are using Truth merely to increase your human good ... increase your weekly income ... remodel your home ... acquire a better automobile ... you have not even TOUCHED the spiritual path.

In each case of the Hebrew prophets, you will notice that their mission was NOT a personal one ... their mission was not just one of human good or just ADDING human good to the world ... it was ALWAYS a SPIRITUAL MISSION.

The same is true of you. YOU have a spiritual mission whether, at this moment, you know it or not. EVERYONE has a spiritual mission and EVERYONE, ultimately, will find it.

ONCE you have entered this spiritual path, there is no way to turn back. You may try it temporarily but you will be driven, forced back into this spiritual path since there IS this, "THOU ART WITH ME."

"Yea, though I walk through the valley of the shadow of death, I will fear no evil, for THOU art with me."

Then it is said, "Thou preparest a table before me in the presence of mine enemies. Thou anointest my head with oil. My cup runneth over."

Here, again, is simply the statement of that which IS. "Thou preparest a table." No affirmation to make it come true ... no petition ... no seeking God ... merely a statement. This is high prayer.

"Thou preparest a table before me in the presence of mine enemies. Thou anointest my head with oil. My cup runneth over."

Then: "SURELY goodness and mercy shall follow me ALL the days of my life!"

How confident he is, "SURELY goodness and mercy... ."

There is another important thought there also: "... ALL the days of my life."

Once you realize that God cannot operate today and not tomorrow, you have touched one of the highest concepts of prayer. If you can acknowledge that at ANY time in your experience you have KNOWN the result of prayer (that is, you have HAD a healing through spiritual means) or if, at any time in your life, you have had an evidence of the presence and power of God ... ACTUALLY ... you should never have to be concerned again because that ONE evidence to you of God's presence should be ENOUGH to make you say, "Surely goodness and mercy shall follow me ALL the days of my life," ALL the days!

How can God be with you today and not tomorrow? How can God manifest or express Itself one day and not the next day?

The Hebrews had a hard time learning that lesson. When they INSISTED on picking manna for tomorrow and the day after and the day after that, Moses had to remind them that if that manna was falling out of the sky by the Grace of God, WHY should they think that it wouldn't fall tomorrow and the day after? Why should God stop as long as there was a need?

Is there a possibility that God will stop your blessings as long as you have a need? Is it possible that the hand of God is shortened or will be withdrawn from you before the fulfillment of your destiny? Why should you ever have to question? Why should you ever have to treat?

Meditate on the spirit of the 23rd Psalm ... a Psalm that in no wise, no place, reaches out to God ... seeks anything from God ... but, rather, rests so completely, so perfectly in the confidence, the assurance, "SURELY goodness and mercy shall follow me ALL the days of my life."

Then comes the conclusion, "And I will DWELL in the house of the Lord forever." "I will dwell" in God consciousness "forever."

There is no treatment about it ... just a statement, "And I will dwell" in God consciousness ... "in the house of the Lord, forever."

That may be a cue for you. Have YOU made the declaration, "I WILL dwell IN the house of the Lord [in God consciousness] forever"?

IF YOU WOULD PRAY

IN THE PASSAGES in *The Infinite Way* (pp. 94–98) reference is made to waking in the morning and then going all through the day in the CONSTANT recognition of the presence and power of God in every experience.

Remember the passages of scripture, "Thou wilt keep him in perfect peace whose mind is STAYED on Thee"; "Acknowledge Him in ALL thy ways and He will give thee rest"; "Quietness and confidence shall be my strength"; "I will DWELL in the house of the Lord forever."

Remember the 91st Psalm, the first verse, "He that DWELLETH in the secret place of the most high." This Psalm goes on to relate the terrible things that would NOT come nigh your dwelling place IF your dwelling place were the secret place of the most high.

Here, again, is the same idea, "I will dwell in the house of the Lord forever."

If YOU are living in the consciousness of God CONSTANTLY, you, too, can say, "The LORD is my Shepherd, I shall not want. He makes me lie down in green pastures. HE leads me beside the still waters...."

If you are NOT living IN the consciousness of the presence of God, certainly you cannot expect to demonstrate the rest of the 91st Psalm or the 23rd Psalm. There again the highest concept or idea of prayer IS the recognition of God as omnipresence and omnipotence ... the recognition of God as ever present, ever available ... the recognition of God as the Law and the Light unto our being, BUT with no attempt to MAKE it so.

THIS is the highest concept of prayer ... this constant DWELLING in the REALIZATION of God-presence.

No longer need you wonder, "What prayer shall I pray today?" You have prayed all the prayer there is when you pray, "I dwell in the house of the Lord now and forever."

Another verification of this is to be found in the 27th Psalm, "The Lord is my light and my salvation; WHOM shall I fear? The Lord is the strength of my life; of whom shall I be afraid? Though an host should encamp against me, my heart shall not fear. Though war should rise against me, in this will I be comforted... . ONE thing have I desired of the Lord ... THAT will I seek after ... THAT I MAY *DWELL* IN THE HOUSE OF THE LORD *ALL* THE DAYS OF MY LIFE."

There it is again. DWELLING, LIVING, MOVING and HAVING YOUR BEING in GOD CONSCIOUSNESS is PRAYER. It is the highest form of prayer there is because once you come to that constant, conscious realization of God, then you come back to your 23rd Psalm and you find you no longer have to reach out to God or pray to God ... you merely say, "Why should I? The Lord IS my shepherd, I shall not want, He MAKETH me to lie down, of course, He MAKETH me as I have made GOD my dwelling place."

This prayer ... this realization of prayer ... is the one that meets ALL of our so-called needs. This is the nature of prayer that reveals our ultimate harmony to us. There is no God sitting around waiting for us to pray in any right manner or wrong manner. There is no God going to suddenly give us something He has been withholding from us.

The Lord being our shepherd, it is IMPOSSIBLE for us to want and it is impossible for God to withhold our good, our safety, our security, our protection; BUT there is a price, and it can be found in the teachings of the Master as well as in the Old Testament.

THAT PRICE IS "Dwelling in the Secret Place of the Most High" ... LIVING in the consciousness of God, forever. That is the answer.

Another confirmation of this can be found in 2 Chronicles 32: "Be strong and courageous. Be not afraid nor dismayed for the King of Assyria ... nor for all the multitude that is with him ... for there be more with us than with him."

There is NO PRAYER, no reaching out to God, no trying to get God to do something. There is merely a STATEMENT.

"With him is an arm of flesh but with us is the Lord our God to help us and to fight our battles."

Then follow the most wonderful words in all scripture, "And the people rested themselves upon the WORDS of Hezekiah."

They didn't rest themselves upon their arms or ammunition, they rested themselves upon the WORDS of Hezekiah, and what were those words? "Be not afraid," the arm of flesh cannot do a thing to you because we have a God.

It is only as we LIVE constantly in that assurance of God's presence that we can say, in the face of any form of trouble, "I will not fear evil, even though I walk through the valley of the shadow of death, because I know Thou art with me. What difference does it make what experience I go through if I am SURE that God is WITH me!"

The one thing to be ever on guard against is the suggestion, through fear, that possibly God is NOT with us.

There is a story about a man who was training his small son. He took him outside, placed him on the first step and said, "Jump into Daddy's arms." The boy jumped and his Daddy caught him.

Then the father placed the boy on the second step and said, "Jump into Daddy's arms." The boy jumped again and his Daddy caught him.

Then the father placed the boy on the third step and said, "Jump into Daddy's arms." The boy jumped, but this time the father let the boy fall. The father explained, "You see, boy, never trust anybody ... not even your Daddy."

Needless to say, after that, the boy could never feel completely assured of his father's help, nor could he know what fatherhood really means.

That is what has happened to us. Somewhere in our lives, through some experience of our own or others, we have come to the conclusion that you cannot depend on Father. When you get to that third step, there is no use trusting Him because He may not be there.

Therefore, it is necessary to go back within the innermost recesses of your own being until you reach that point of conviction that the Father IS present ... that you do not have to fear the multitudes ... that you do not even have to FEAR while you are in the valley of the shadow of death ... that you need have no FEAR of lack and limitation even in the presence of your enemies.

"Thou preparest a table before me in the presence of mine enemies. Yea, though I walk through the valley of the shadow of death" I cannot be made to fear even then, since "Thou art with me."

If you would attain the highest concept of prayer, you must stop praying in the ordinary sense of WORDS. Make your prayer a CONTINUOUS REALIZATION of the presence and power of God in ALL your ways. Twenty-four hours a day KNOW that God is guiding and directing your EVERY thought, word and deed. LIVE in a constant remembrance of your beloved Father.

ENTER THE SILENCE

SILENCE IS POWER. Silence is the healing activity in individual consciousness. Silence is the creative Principle of all existence.

In this Silence, you become receptive to the Inner Voice, the Voice of the Inner Self, and as Truth expresses Itself in your listening ear, you become aware of the Healing Influence, with signs following.

Your receptivity to the Kingdom of God, God Consciousness, God Awareness, God Knowing, constitutes a healing atmosphere.

Heretofore, the work of the student has been to bring about harmony in his experience through the statement or affirmation of Truth, or reading or quoting Truth. Now he rises higher in consciousness to where he constantly and consciously "listens" for Truth to utter Itself within him. He learns the true nature of Silence, of stillness and quietness.

It is easy to understand why the sages of old taught, "Be still, and know that I am God"; that this stillness declares the Presence of God, "Closer than breathing, nearer than hands and feet." It reveals that neither man nor circumstance nor condition can be power over your affairs, since that which declared Itself to be "I" within you is God, is Power, is Presence.

Also, you now know why you can never be God but that God is inseparable from your very being. All this reveals itself to you in The Silence.

Always remember that it is not the thoughts you think nor the truths you read, but rather, That which has revealed Itself in "quietness and confidence" is God, the Restorer of Harmony in your existence. It is not the thoughts you think but the thoughts which unfold to you within your own being ... these constitute your guidance and inner wisdom. It is not so much the thoughts of Truth you declare, as the consciousness of Truth you develop through your inner receptivity, that brings God-government into your body and outer affairs.

The activity of Truth in your consciousness is the Light which dispels the darkness of human sense. It is not what you think about

Truth but what Truth knows and declares to you ... not what you affirm to Divine Mind but what It reveals to you. This is The Silence. This is Power.

In quietness and confidence, in stillness and Silence, Love reveals Its comforting Presence and assures us that "underneath are the everlasting arms" upholding and supporting us, even in trial and tribulation.

The heading over the 23rd Psalm is "David's confidence in God's grace." Can you not feel this calm confidence as you read, "The Lord is my Shepherd; I shall not want." Here there is no petition, no supplication and, above all, no doubt or fear. Since the Lord IS his Shepherd, HOW can he want?

"He maketh me to lie down in green pastures; He leadeth me beside the still waters." (The peace that passeth understanding enfolds me as I realize I cannot escape from my good, since He not only provides me with green pastures but He MAKETH me to lie down in them; He not only gives me still waters but He LEADETH me beside the still calm waters of peace.)

"He restoreth my soul." (Even though it has been scarlet with sin or unrestful in sickness, yet "He restoreth my soul; He leadeth me in the paths of righteousness for His name's sake," and though I still be tempted with desire, yet for His name's sake He leadeth me out of sin into righteousness, out of disease into rightness of health.)

"Yea, though I walk through the valley of the shadow of death, I will fear no evil, for Thou art with me; Thy rod and Thy staff they comfort me." (David's confidence in God's grace is still felt, even in the valley of the shadow of death, since even here David feels no fear, "for Thou art with me." Oh, God, that I too may "be still" and know no fear, since even in the valley of the shadow of death "Thou art with me.")

You can only experience fear if you believe that, in the midst of your discords and inharmonies, God has deserted you. NEVER, in scarlet sin nor dangerous disease, will you fear, once you attain David's confidence that even in the valley of the shadow of death "Thou art with me." Let the Beloved Silence descend upon you, too, as you realize with all your being that "Thou art with me."

"Thy rod and Thy staff they comfort me." (God's grace, always manifest in the human form of rod, staff, food or water, this grace appearing as my good, comforts me. This assurance of the presence of that which fulfills, protects, sustains ... this comforts me.)

"Thou preparest a table before me in the presence of mine enemies; Thou anointest my head with oil; my cup runneth over." (Where lack and limitation threaten, God's grace prevails; my soul is filled with inspiration and my heart overflows with joy and gratitude. This evidence of abundance, through Grace, fills me ... satisfies me ... and my heart sings for joy in His Presence.)

"Surely goodness and mercy shall follow me all the days of my life and I will dwell in the House of the Lord forever." (How confident, how positive is David, as he sings, "Surely goodness and mercy shall follow me," and how secure he feels in the timelessness of God's Grace, as he declares that this goodness and mercy "shall follow me all the days of my life." Blessed assurance of Omnipresence, "ALL the days of my life." And, of course, "I will dwell in this consciousness of God forever. Yes, God Consciousness shall be my home forever.")

"The former things have passed away" and "All things are become new." "Whereas I was blind, now I see" and not "through a glass, darkly" but "face to face." Yes, even in my flesh I have seen God. The hills have rolled away and there is no more horizon but the light of heaven makes all things plain.

Long have I sought Thee, O Jerusalem, but only now have my pilgrim feet touched the soil of heaven. The waste places are no more. Fertile lands are before me, the like of which I have never dreamed. Oh, truly, "There shall be no night there." The glory of it shines as the noonday sun. There is no need of light, for God is the light thereof.

I sit down to rest. In the shade of trees I rest and find my peace in Thee. Within Thy Grace is peace, O Lord. In the world I was weary, in Thee I have found rest. In the dense forest of words I was lost, in the letter of Truth was tiredness and fear ... but in Thy Spirit ONLY is shade and water and rest.

How far have I wandered from Thy Spirit, O Tender One and True, how far, how far. How deeply lost I have been in the maze of words ... words ... words. But now am I returned, and in Thy Spirit shall I ever find my life, my peace, my strength. Thy Spirit is the Bread of Life, finding which, I shall never hunger again. Thy Spirit is a well-spring of water, drinking which, I shall never thirst again.

As a weary wanderer I have sought Thee and now my weariness is gone. Thy Spirit has formed a tent for me, and in its cool shade I linger. Peace fills my soul. Thy Presence has filled me with peace. Thy love has placed before me a Feast of Spirit. Yes, Thy Spirit is my resting place, an oasis in the desert of the letter of Truth.

In Thee will I hide from the noise of the world of argument, in Thy Consciousness find surcease from the noisomeness of men's tongues. They divide Thy Garment, O Lord of Peace, they quarrel over Thy Word until It becomes words and no longer Word.

As a beggar have I sought the new heaven and the new earth, and Thou hast made me heir of all. How shall I stand before Thee but in Silence? How shall I honor Thee but in the MEDITATION of my heart?

Praise and thanksgiving Thou seekest not, but the understanding heart Thou receivest. I will keep silent before Thee. My Soul and my Spirit and my Silence shall be Thy Dwelling Place. Thy Spirit shall fill my meditation, and It shall make me and preserve me whole. O Tender One and True, I am Home in Thee.

Made in the USA
San Bernardino, CA
31 December 2017